SMALL AS A RESURRECTION

Grateful acknowledgment is made to the following
publications in which these poems first appeared:

Coastlight: "Oppenheimer," "Japanese Box," "Bluffout,"
    "Reading the Journals of Kokan"
Ironwood: "To Make A Narcissus Into A Machine"
The Massachusetts Review: "Preparing the Silk"
Three Rivers Poetry Journal: "Ninja"

Library of Congress Cataloging in Publication Data

Johnson, Honor
    Small as a resurrection

    (Lost Roads series : no. 20)
    I. Title
PS3560.03784S6 1983   811'.54   82-82498
ISBN 0-918786-23-1

Published by Lost Roads Publishers
PO Box 310 Eureka Springs, AR 72632
First Printing 1983 by Wheeler Printing

Cover: *Tollund, The Broken Pitcher,* intaglio by Wayne Johnson
Book Design by Forrest Gander and C.D. Wright

This project is supported by a grant from the National
Endowment for the Arts in Washington, D.C., a federal agency.

To My Friends

CONTENTS

Honor Johnson
SMALL AS A RESURRECTION

Lost Roads
Number 20   1983
San Francisco — Eureka Springs

I

OPPENHEIMER

Swept up by power we say and summon some inane image of sweeping
tirelessly endlessly where everything remains unswept. . .
His horse's tail makes this sound as he rides through moonlight watching
lightning hit the forest and he smiles
wants to take the more dangerous path
to the other atomic scientists' horror but secret admiration.
In my mind he looks Japanese, small but lithe
and he has the classical Japanese face too
almond-shaped long through the center with a small
intelligent mouth.

When the hooves crack into the town he tries to sell the story
that they are working on electric rockets
but there is no interest.
No one will come over to spy, there are no curious Russians.
It is not like the Jimmy Stewart movies it is almost disappointing.
And yet one worn farmer says when the rain fell the hair of his cows
came out, grew back in spots so he was sure
this was something atomic.

People in Alamogordo drank a lot threw hard parties, just like the
normals.
There with their uncertain smiles, their square-cut dresses and suits
one would have thought at a glance they were no different.
The cat joins my lap as I see the photographs of them
working on FATMAN with a tape measure
it strikes me as ridiculous.
The cat looks away from the screen towards the kitchen door
bored with anything that is not a cue
my nervous hands tangle in his coat.
The bomb blast itself was purple and green the color of bruises.

On looking back he is not sure why they did not stop here, stop here.
Chevalieur is shown, and his brother, neither has
eyes that lock quite like his.
It is rumoured he was hard on his students.

A friend in Berkeley calls, his voice creaks through the telephone
"Did you know my roommate Jim yes that's the one the Marxist, he was
periodically discouraged, angry." Last year this same friend had
read me a poem. It sounded like Octavio Paz. "Jim is dead, he committed
suicide last Thanksgiving day. He had been in a wreck the week before
with a minor concussion. The doctors were giving him tranquilizers
they didn't know about his history of attempted suicide. It was just
the day before the nuclear protests. . . ."

I wanted to get back to the television. The program before the Atomic
Scientists was the history of dinosaurs, the great Cretaceous dieoff
shown in cartoons. The computer-simulated Tyrannosaurus Rex flashes
     back at me
like a jingly commercial that wouldn't fade.
"He had gone to the old place in the park where he had been stealing
stone to carve, with a note in his pocket. It was me they called and I
had to call everyone even his parents. They wanted to go to
court but I stopped them."

Back to my place on the couch where I like to sit and stare at the T.V.
I didn't miss the program. It is the same defensive position that I took in
     Austin
when the two girls were murdered in the shower and their murderer was
     not found,
A good position when alone, it allows me to have a sweep of the house. By
     my side
is an article from *Omni*: quarks, after all just pictures and not an
     explanation.
Three Quarks for Mr. Mark. An ad for *Kagemusha* at the local Palo Alto
     theater.

This photograph of Oppenheimer looks like a Nō Play Mask. Leaning
     down, ghostly white,
it is as if it were taken by an electron scanner. For a moment it looks as if
his face is a nest of tissue holding malignant bacteria. I always thought him
     absolutely
beautiful. I hated the McCarthy era. Now I see him in a more natural way.

After Hiroshima he and the others went into the blast site to find evidence.
No one hated them, they were surprised, as if they had punched through a
     barrier

10

they thought was lead and it was cotton. One of them brought back a wall burned
with the shadow of window frame, the curtains, the blinds, and the little pull
string all marked with the angle at which the bomb went off.
They sat down to study it just a few feet from the old women and the blinded.

JAPANESE BOX

Before the Second World War a workman
garotted that iris in your oxblood lacquer sky.
For pennies my mother's inquisitive fingernails
slit you with a click.

After her life closed you are American summer nights
brown photographs, the foul smell of powderpuffs.
A cobra iris has lost its hood and drifts
in vagueness.
How finite can a world be?

You are Canopic jars.
One paint thin plant
flaking.
Nostalgia of old desire.

In your past her dry face drifts like rust
ridiculous in the light of her conclusion.
After a life is over it is small.
Where does used powder go?

Sex is a mechanical bird that calls out "Over"
"Over." A window
where small heads emerge. A dark brown butterfly
it falls and slides on shellac.

In you my father's childhood eyeglasses.
He might have been a genius.
Later this serpent-toothed ring, its green quartz
his broken tooth,
a warbling watch.

All digested, all stung with poison.
There's a light of pretense in your lid
when the top's down
flat as a cat's mouth.

An anatomy demonstration.

I would say "boxes and boxes to the end of the world."
My grandmother at her end showed me how small
places were "That small, that small" she said
remembering with her fingers.
The black dragon beard on your lock looks petulant.
It is not the devil but almost.

I find an ivory-circled cameo
of my mother with a teddy bear, she didn't like this picture.
Kohara took it, she said it made her look slant-eyed, Japanese.
She looks down with the delicate childlike air she always had

And probably says things that turn the stomach.
Her baggy trousers are pure indigo
like the milk of magnesia bottle.
What could she know of lies in lies in lies?

ARS POETICA

1. After the lovers with no partners
   have all called softly to death
   and some one has seen the very thin people
   walking up the side of the hill,
   after you finish your conversation on John Locke
   and who owns water in the Mojave in the afternoon
   and the stars have flocked out
   behind the pelvis of the rocks
   I tell you of the time in Texas
   when we had the year of the rattlesnake.
   At first the water came
   and then the grain did well,
   then came mice and insects
   and boys got their B-B guns
   and shot rats off the rafters
   and after that the rattlesnakes;
   so bad you couldn't step off the porch.

2. Do you notice how the tracks of sidewinders
   are like Greek written in the sand.
   And their mouths unhinge at the side,
   skeptical, as the French are.
   Mouths like Voltaire.
   Tragedy a dried gray branch in the sand.
   A list of alphabets that never merged into speech.

3. The child learned to play with a gourd in her cradle
   and later she went out to her father's radio shack
   and picked up a nest of rattlesnakes.
   When her father found her she was giggling.
   Kitty, her sister, and I took the snakes
   and made little wire nooses for their bodies.
   Waving the dead snakes behind us we walked back and forth
   up the street
   and waited for our parents' friends to stop their cars and try to
   save us.

IN LOUISIANA

there is no stock law.
My Uncle Pete is driving to Marksville in the rain.
There are deep red gouges in the road
filled with black water.
Suddenly a cow walks out of the pine forest.
Pete turns the wheel as best he can
but the cow bashes his dark blue car and slides along the hood
until she hits the windshield, then she
breaks through and hits his youngest son in the mouth
and knocks out his front teeth.
Rickey, the son, doesn't want false teeth
and for a while they can't get him to keep the bridge in.
He says other boys play football and have lost teeth.
Even when his rival cousin has his nose straightened
Rickey does not get teeth.
Then Rickey does get teeth, but he won't get braces
and a piece of his cut lip still hangs down in front
and he won't change that.
He has a handsome strong face but it looks a little battered
and he won't get the piece of skin cut off.
His mother nags him as she nagged him about getting fat
and he won't.
In Louisiana medicine is bad.
Every year the construction company sends my Uncle Pete in for a
physical but they don't treat his blood pressure.
One night he goes into the bathroom and falls across the
threshold
as he is coming back.
His wife runs to him but he can't answer.
The ambulance comes.
I go with Rickey to the hospital, St. Francis Cabrini.
We sit there in the waiting room, no one speaks to me.
I have on old clothes and my mother has chopped my hair off.
Rickey is unhappy, the piece of skin is trembling.
He is afraid his father is dead and no one comes to talk to him.
They kind of move away.

I say I will go and see but I can't find out anything.
In Louisiana doctors do not talk to the family.
They stand hangdog at the door and look at the kids.
If the woman of the family is not there they wander off,
if she is they shake their heads and leave.
Now they put him on an airplane and fly him to Houston.
He is terrified, they don't even ask so they don't know.
His blue eyes don't twinkle anymore.
Dr. DeBakey operates on him, the heart doctor
who is followed by rows of other surgeons like rows of ducks.
He says Pete has an aneurism in his right kidney
and it will move up to the heart if they don't operate.
It works, Pete is taken home.
It takes him two years to die.
He lies on his bed staring at the ceiling.
His vision is going, he can't see his children.
And his wife turns away now, she wants him to die.
Rickey won't let anyone cut away the flesh on his lip
and the family gangs up on him about it.

TO MAKE A NARCISSUS INTO A MACHINE

1. Once Wayne and I wandered into a French toy shop
and he bought a white wooden toy
le oiseau qui vole.
Many wings and whirring at once.
We ate afterwards from folded napkins.
Time stopped (like a superimposed drawing)
and the wings were everywhere.

2. Imagine a convent.
The nuns want gargoyles for water.
It rains only on the north half of the sky
so on the south side of the nunnery
they build arched waterspouts.
"God makes the water holy
on its way from the south side to the north."
But from the high perfect fountains
there comes perfume, not water.
Then one midnight one of the nuns
discovers that the gargoyles
are wimples of her sisters
hung high on the walls.

3. Here in Japan
we take the fine paper off our fans.
This exposes the bamboo sticks
which stand upright, together
but not in a fan shape.
The Zen Master says forget the paper.
Many stalks for one flower,
quoting an English woman.
But there is still paper
torn and furled, at the end of each stalk.
This is called the Narcissus Ceremony.

A THING I MIGHT DO

In the park there is a game called the kite game.
First we lie out on the road and someone with a steam roller
flattens us out, makes us sticky.

Then children come with feathers, they feather especially
the space under the arms and between the thighs.

When we are wide as we are tall we are lifted to our feet.
A woman lifts the skin from our spines.
It is painless.

She inserts a mile of pale blue string.

We line up one after the other. Villagers come out
at first hesitant, then they take the ropes.

We twirl in a long line like many envelopes or many pieces of
paper.
Some of us right side up and some of us upside down.
Some become excited and twirl over and over and some of us
flap at the waist or match our edges or make accordians.

We are all situated with our heads looking the same direction,
out into the blue.

Because of the winds no one hears the child with a torch
who touches the mother strings.

Pink Floyd starts and I began to dance at first slowly
but then jerking my head and arms as if they belonged to a
puppet.
Over the dog's head I roll my black and white Russian sleeves
and he looks up, and cocks his head and then rises to join me.
Skillfully because he intends to bite my wrists
I lead him to the right and left of me, dancing to him and away.
And his attempt to bite me on the sleeves is subverted,
slowed, smiling in profile, the indirect
full smile of a dog.
He is as big as I am, the music turns to John Lennon,
still we dance now, he is up on his hind legs, his
delicate wolf ankles clicking.
He smiles and bites playfully at a place over my heart
which I keep just out of his reach, Old Ethics
Old Aesop Animal; he would look, in a bonnet,
like the French Revolution.
We turn in tight circles, his smoke tail
wagging a little, our steps crossing like the fox trot.
His smile is between aggression and desire,
little pink spots on the sides of his lips
show as we turn in our mazurka, towards the gray light
of windows that etch lines in my hands and neck.
I think of lighting candles on my table
red for love, green for money, next to freesias.
Like Leonardo's angels he is always in profile.
His teeth a clamp that just misses my wrist.
I am skillful, skillful, how I manipulate this
to keep it light, prolong the pleasure.

I AM WALKING

through Brooklyn
and a young man thinks he knows who I am.
Vaguely I recognize him, vaguely
he is my friend Carl. But made shining
all shining. I stop because the light from him
will not let go my face. He is the color
of a mango, sliced and held.
His mind is everywhere in his body.
He tells me nothing.
His smile is three leaves that break
like chalk in my hands.

The old man is big and vague, his body
swings like so many sacks in his muscles.
He smells of too many meals with sausages,
not that he had them, that he smiled through
them. Now he smiles at me with short pig teeth.
It is difficult for me to know
how right he is, how much I am like him
because when I think of it
all beauty vanishes from me.

I meet the older woman, I don't notice
that she is old. She has made herself over
not to look young, but to look taut.
She sits rodlike, smiles artificially
but I forgive her this. As I sit down
she begins to relax and as she does so
everything the surgeons have done comes undone.
She turns to me and says
"It's been so long. It's been a long hard time."
I put my arm on her shoulder and
we begin to weep.

I meet the younger woman, she is part German.
Her mouth is enormous and she is eating ice cream with men.

They don't want me to join since most of their pleasure
is in being with this woman. She sees this, she pulls over
a chair for me and everyone smiles compliantly.
She says that I am interesting, and that I would
look good as a nude dancer, she knows just the kind
of nude dancer. I smile, beginning to lose myself
begin to believe her.

The tree is there dancing with leaves of silver, dancing
slippers.
No, they break off and fall like leaves. It turns in front of me
shivers as if laughing and as I reach out to touch
it drifts back.

BLUFFOUT

1. My poor cousin
I used to call you Horse
when I was in a good mood. Four times
as a child you stuck your fingers in the light sockets
your flesh turned blue at the nails
the doctor couldn't get you to stop.
Now you can't stay married.
I have a teacher with a giant's face like yours.
He takes offense too easily but I like his German giant look.
He has long red hands like my mother's red slippers
worn through the palms.
The bones in them seem to collapse.
Men were your saviors, Gene Autrey and television.
Fishing trips a life away
from a mother who was damned and saved by everything.
She was more afraid of men than I am
her body smelled of rotten carrots.
I have that blue handkerchief she carried
when we took you into the dogwood forest
and you found black mushrooms
ran to us saying "Turds, turds."
I didn't know you could say anything but Momma.
You slept with your thumb in your mouth
and your ass in the air.

The teacher says Death is a different thing every day
sometimes German, sometimes apples
and sometimes summerripe or underripe.

Danish, his face pointed like Kierkegaard's, he watches
a chalk mark on the blackboard
where a white horse knocks up clods of dirt in a deep meadow.
It's hung with oranges, the kind in Meeker, that never get ripe.
Death is not like that in my opinion.
He won't let my mother talk, he laughs
at her fear of doctors
won't tell her the results of his examinations.

All three of you want to be alone so it won't hurt anymore.
Like the old mean man that ran the ferris wheel
compelled to give endless demonstrations
of how to run us backwards till we screamed out.

2. My grandfather whom you look like
splayed his paws over his fig trees.
Took out walnut meats with a blade.
"Squirrel brains" he whispered.
His wife read St. Augustine.
I was in the rodeo carrying flowers for Jesus
when he died like a deerskin returned from the cleaners.
I was eight. I went into hysterics.
Death was such an awful embarrassment.

There was a race of Apes that laughed like that
in my favorite book, *John Carter of Barsoom*.

Like him our grandfather travels to Mars.
Turns his big body to me in vague light
and says he sees white horses here
just boys here
but when he tries to ride they have all gone.
He asks about Joe his blind nag
I describe his slow gait. I eat figs.

Which turn into my thumb as I wake.

3. My father was a cook during the war in France.
Street children came to stare at the Americans
he wanted to give them chocolate but the Nazis
passed out poison bars.
The kids said *chok o lot* they were hungry.
Sometimes he gave them knuckles of mutton
but they threw them away.

And as he was walking there was
a boy like you   dead   out by the apples.

My father never wanted a girl child.
In this time of hysteria
he had forgotten my mother's face.
In America he taught you to play baseball.
He didn't even like me to watch.
At home when I tried to talk to him
he usually gave me a hostile sermon
on what was good and bad.

How many times did I lure you into the cesspool
throw the football there and watch your body sink
into the soft dichondra
just your hand waving back to me
and your compulsion to smile.

SONG TO CALL THE SOUL BACK

the limbs of the plum tree
are broken and gone
one yellow bird stays on call him oriole
he is an utterly still bone shadow
and if he isn't gone
and if he isn't gone
his body is dark and black
because he is in shade
the fruit of the plum tree
is colder yellow
sour as his wings
hop said the old woman
as if she gave commands
his two branch limbs
one yellow plum
and she lives under a hill
hating the sour light
hating the sour light

SONG OF THE NEAR DIVORCED

a man and a woman
lived in an oven
and they made flutes
from black and white goats
the pair of them moved
in remarkable rhythm
through fields of flowers
through pale gold flowers
and they learned each other
they hated each other
but they didn't know it
they never knew it
one night he gave her
the skin of the moon
the black and white moon
the tough little woman
tried to apologize
but the sky was so angry
the sun was so angry
the backbone of the moon
rocked on the horizon
rocked on the horizon
knuckled the earth
and when the man
was in the field plowing
he fell in the hole
he died in the hole
then later that night
the moon took his stomach
his middle aged stomach
put it in the oven
and started the fire
the woman burned too
the woman burned too
it's part of the tale
that the woman burn too

THE TEACHER

The old man was from the kennel club and he came to drop something
off for Shadow. He spoke very slowly and walked with a limp. I sat
him in the living room with me and waited until he pulled out a
long silver leash and the kind of collar called a training
collar, with spikes inside that stick into the throat when the
leash is pulled. "This will help you in your teaching," he
said. And slipped the noose over Bill's neck, being careful to
shield the eyes with his hands. His hands were silky and marked
with liver spots. The leash itself was very decorative and the
collar made of gold fig leaves. Bill began to read one of his
poems. The old man smiled very encouragingly, yet every once in a
while he gave a strong pull on the leash. Bill looked mortally
insulted but the old man kept chanting in a high voice, "That was
splendid, that was just splendid."

II.

Epitaphs

SUSPENSION

I was drawing the lily pond, the whole thing, frogs, pads, blossoms
and light on water. I captured each one with a line as it faded
as the white paper recurred, shining, shining through its flesh.

THOUGHT

Turning from the porcelain Buddha in the Brundage collection
I was struck with the falling in his opiate sleep, his beautiful mouth
and wondered if when this moment came you would hear the rattling in
my eyes.

TOTEN TANZ

We waded into the swamp. His German face the same awake and sleeping.
Ice springs and briars. Yellow leaves floated away.
The pressure of his flesh made blackberries crush in the red
haze.

THE END OF THE VIKINGS

It was so simple. We went out that morning with some candles
we had made the night before, tall with long wicks, and we burned them
in sunlight until the light filled us, filled all the ice.

FOR MY TOMBSTONE

If you still insist that you love me go to the mouth of Baillet's Lake.
The spring clay is veined red and blue. Make clay apples and a clay pitcher.
Place them to dry on the path next to you where the cottonmouths sun.

FOR MY TOMBSTONE (2)

I looked at all of you in that light that did not cast shadows,
followed your delicate features, your excellence, I thought
time bent at this moment and I could follow my own light touch out to the
fields.

PREPARING THE SILK

its a sand colored day   perfectly even
no trees in an open courtyard
no one looks at the cashew walls
lit with a wash not even a matchglow out of place
the weavers have gently carried cocoons off the mulberry
gutted them with skillful hands leaving a smash of blood
among leaves
now long slender fingers wash in a bowl
the thread has gone from linear to solid
its thick and right
you pull it and the surface doesnt give
what a display of calm noon life
now its delivered to the women
they attach it to a scroll
one sings
they do it leisurely
with long sure turns of their butterfly napes
they do what is left to do   what involves art
the one in cerulean and peach
puts the left end on a stick
then the right one
this is so it will fold
no matter what is written there
at any moment it can be returned to silence
the one in cream and blue mountains
turns the right and pulls it taut
another one irons the surface using heated sizing
beeswax and poisons
stop the paint
the heat turns the fibers in one direction
sizing made from bird bones and sticks of plum
a little girl
whom it has taken three hours to dress in peony silk
squats under it
turns her head in an artificial way
like a white crane
it is her job to let no light through

Oct. 11: Sue says she was a Phi Delta and that there were women telling
        her all
night and part of the next night that the black man who brought her to the
dorms would ruin her in the organization. Their mean cigarette-smoking
faces pressed into the wooden ceiling and stayed there. The next year,
without any possessions, she was on a North American freighter. Only
        when it
started to move did she learn that it was going to Capetown. Mid-Atlantic
the moon turned red.
                I am having trouble with my side as she talks. I
strain to breathe and my lungs escape like old silk gloves waving goodbye to
everyone. Maybe it's the old sorority hatred, I don't know. As the bus
turns the corner I read,
                        "The diameter of the world is more than seven
thousand miles and the sea route circumnavigating it is over twenty-four
thousand. The most distant region of the West is called Europe." You with
your perfect Japanese manners going to the far side of the world. To see
what is real, to see what is not pretended.
                When I try to breathe it hurts. Nothing, but I
feel as if it is a predeath. You say this continent could contain several
thousand Japans.

All night blossoms in Capetown windows. Jasmine predates the settlers and
        will outlast them. The air is made of sulphuric acid and gold. The
        people are selfish old mirrors that eat.

                        "In Japan we call all Western painting 'Dutch
        painting'."

My mother writes a little note which says that a young girl should always be
encouraged to smile, always encouraged to be happy.

Oct. 12: Jackie Winsor does a piece I see in *Art News*. She does balls of
        twine in copper. From a distance they look like balls of twine.

The piece is said to be a container of energy. All night pain can be held off
        as if a person very skilled in martial arts were combatting it.

One of the works is called Burnt Piece.

Oct. 13: You are struck with the need for perfect detail. It is to know: to
  gather together.
The people of Ambodia preserved a mermaid in embalming fluid and drew
  pictures of her. Now you say after so many years the mermaid is no
  longer perfect, but we know what she first looked like. You saw the
  pictures.

For the love of God I am in my fortieth year. I have earlier photographs.
  Western books use pictures for supplemental description.
Imagine Westerners with their dark hats and strange noses, looking for
  mushrooms.
They make no mistakes. Because of the pictures no one is poisoned.

All things depicted in pictures, from the great wild goose to the tiny sparrow
but not the reality of social interaction.
No one does that.

Oct. 14: When you were young a Hollander arrived in the port of Japan
  carrying copperplate. No one would buy. The Japanese thought they
  were superior.

She said something happened to the moon when she crossed the cape.
Red but not near the horizon.
The water was bloodstreaked.
"We entered Capetown in a corridor."
She sat on the deck in her perfect American dress.
In the same space of time I was in America feeling contaminated, outcast,
  foreign.
I would have thought there was no risk leaving a loveless house.

Oct. 15: To make. To bring into being. To prepare for use.
I understand now looking in her face that she had no need for anyone to
  understand her. At that time everyone wanted her. Her best use for
  them (like the Japanese geographers) was for her maps.

"The life of man passes in a twinkling
Life is a running white horse seen through a chink in the door"

Oct 15: The worm in the peach is a peach worm.
The worm in the chestnut is a chestnut worm.
The worm that lives in the earth is a man.
Worms, worms from the nobles down
eat, copulate, and crepidate.

Johannesburg was completely different and she did not understand why
there was not already revolution there.

Oct 18: When one makes pigment it is sometimes good to make a perfect
red although there are more restrictive ways of working. They are called
red reserving. Not a slightly rusty leaf although the shape of the maple
leaf contributes to its color. Not the oversweet of the raspberry. Not
the coral flash of the flamingo.

It occurred to Sue that deep in the night people were white or dark or yellow
on the outside, but on the inside, red. Like elephant plums.

Oct 19: "Monkey boy, the peddler of foreign pictures." Arrogant
fabricator. The maker of copperplate.

In Cuba she was call *puta*.
They did not like her opinions but knew me for mine. As a knife knows its
diseases.
It was clear they wanted to let the organization live through her.

Scorned me so hard they made my hands tremble.

The city and its dark chimneys. Tall. Storks here in summer. They live in
Europe. Walk in circles. I wonder how many times I have glided
around the house as they glide around the Nile. Catch my feet on
things. There is no pride in walking. Foot slammed down like empty
hand.

Emptiness makes a slapping sound.

In Wales I was called Elizabeth for my soft breathing.

I did not understand machines. I thought the steam engine was not
important. I thought precision couldn't pass beyond a person. Perfect
facility in the space of the day.

Oct 20: This is a beautiful, beautiful day. I am thinking of a deep dream a trip to the islands. She asks me to remember the gauzy Indies light. I remember the Port of Havana with spars raised everywhere; the feeling that I was caught in a soft melon covered web.

I brought back fans.

Another bad night, as if a disease is progressing. I am not loved. Why so ignored? There is nothing I can draw out of these walls no matter how I press my hand to them.

You have copied the true shape of the sun. This picture from a Dutch book is the Japanese sun seen over the sea in a dark mirror. The edge resembles a spray of sea waves blown back by a strong wind.

So small you cup your hands and a crown appears inside. I dream of the noise of a firing bullet. Circle of flames around the pistol nose.

Sue calls on the telephone. I am relieved, we talk not about theories but about a long-legged solid dog.

I wait for the sound and the feeling of water.

Oct 21: There are two readers, two kinds. One makes too much of ornament, complains and goes to pain inside. The other is a child with lively sensations. You want him to want more. I want him to die.

For a cicada life lasts eighty days or so. From summer to autumn the following year when a new cicada finds the sunrise. Newly created. The life of a gnat is two hours.

Driving the car I think of harsh zaps of light that disassemble my body then put it back together again. Would it be me?
No.
But maybe like the color red in all red things.   No.
Universals that decay.

Noon in the car mirror. No telephone.

Oct. 22: You notice that sulphur burns underground just as charcoal burns. Maybe the whole inside of the earth is yellow.

Oct 24: You say that no one in Japan understands the rotation of the earth.

I draw when my depression does not make it impossible. Sometimes things at the edge of the canvas go off. An unpleasant effect. Space wrenched like a squinting eye. I wipe with a rag and the paint remembers and holds on to an emotion. Russia you say is located to the north. The Russians know very little but you are sure that the Russians think of us as animals.

I draw people as animals. Legs and arms cut loose. Polished wood. Chair legs. Sue contributes some of her European dolls. I like their small hands and handmade shoes.

The theory of evolution does not work. No one just sewed dolls together. A natural order. More cunning. Somewhere back in the earth is a memory.

It is cold as an old woman who hurts too much.
Reptiles first, then fine shoes.

The first speaker said, "Do not copy." They straightened their hardback chairs. The Japanese learned what girls do here, convention and decoration. Hard you told yourself. Be hard. That is why it hurts walking round the house. The shock.

Oct 25: Of tobacco the first time a person smokes he feels dizzy. "If a bird or an insect eats tobacco it dies immediately."
"It doth require to be purged with fire
think of this when you smoke tobacco."
Bad habits floating up from the plants in the South.

She tells of the time the company came to get the smallpox victims. No vaccinations. One woman stood over her children and moaned. "All that work and no vaccinations!"

Etching is done with a needle. One first spreads the metal with beeswax and then one makes a design through lines and precise harsh marks represent shadows.

These you took back to your country
Wale fishing off Greenland
A narwhale
The stalk flowers and seeds of saffron
Peach branches and round wormy fruit

Sue and I find my mother's *Life* magazine with a picture of Neil Armstrong
and a picture of the moon on the cover. It has been thumbed. The
moon is fine white porcelain thumbed with smallpox.

You try to explain to your country
Planet
Parallax
Satellite
have no translation in Japanese.

I wonder if my mother was at all proud of me. One doesn't know such
things. Your heir Tarzan was very honest but not particularly cultured.
An embarrassment. I have no children because I am afraid of
Caesareans. Sue because it would interrupt her travels.

Insects seen clearly through a microscope. One can see their eyes, their
feelings. "Western women have very long noses and white
complexions. Though they are extremely beautiful they never smile."

A basket maker, waterfowl, waterflow. . . .

My hands shake with fear of people.
I had a passionate longing for fame and wealth. . . in pursuit of this I. . .

A dream of old dogs sitting in a sewing basket.

"I took a map of the world and explained it.
A woman of about 36 was listening, drew close to me, and said that she
understood from my explanation where the historical Buddha Shaka
lived in India but she wanted to know where Paradise is, for she hoped
she could go there alive."

THE TURNS

1. What is the difference?
Suppose I were the mosquito woman,
I would gauge my beauty differently.
Celebrate everything delicate.
Small bones would be enough
and whispers
and the smooth sea of the human body.

2. There is a story in which a Japanese woman
did not kill the beetles who ate
her warrior husband's face
and then came to tell her of his death.
Perhaps vengeance is inappropriate
when too much of the victim has entered the victor.

3. There are beetles, certain beetles
that roll dung into balls and carry it
like people collecting postage stamps or pieces of string.
Elegantly dressed insects, sometimes shimmering green.
A woman in the art museum represents death
by a thin kimono the color of the ocean.

NINJA

Okada
when you said last night after my performance
that my belly was like a soft white puppy
bouncing in silk cloth
and that you had never seen a woman move like that
I was afraid you guessed.
You did not see me stiffen and look at you
through long eyes.
You said you loved me and intended
to support me
and I felt touched.
It reminded me of the time
we danced through Japanese lanterns
and I caught my fingernails to the back of your neck
when I learned I could not be your wife
but you would be pleased to have me otherwise.
You said my face was beautiful like a water animal's
you said like a delicate lizard.
You didn't see my jaw thrust or know
what I had been counting on.
I went home and took
the slim stick with the chain
buried inside
and the rope that folds to nothing
and came back to your house
dancing in the same way
my stomach bobbing in the water
as I swam with my thighs
moving them as if there was
a man between them.
Then I slithered through the long grass
until your friend and gatesman came
out into the long grass of the yard.
Until I was close enough I pretended
I was a stone.
Do not look for him.

Someone may have seen me then.
I do not look like a woman
when I am working.
There is a tight black hood
over most of my face
and I wear loose-fitting clothes
tied with bows like a hunter would wear.
In them are foodstuffs weapons and poison
sometimes in a bracelet.
You have beautiful moonflowers in your garden.
I stood under the bush for hours
with the blossoms hanging and bobbing
around and over my face.
I was taken for one of the dark branches near the heart.
Because of what I put on my body
your dogs did not stop.
I put a fire
next to the door
where your son slept.
The men found it and tried to put it out with water.
It only smoked.
They became furious and blamed one another.
I told the boy we were playing a game.
He laughed
and allowed me to fasten the cloth
over his head.
I have trouble pulling things taut but he went limp quickly.
There was nothing to take from the house
but on the way out
I startled some quail in the ginkos.
When the men came I walked on my hands
into a dark shed
careful not to touch anyone.
There were servants sleeping in there.
No one was pretending.
I crawled out like a bent crab
and plunged into the water.
My hair came loose and part of my clothing.

I was anxious to finish.
I live nearby I will not tell you where.
When I reached this place
I hired a man to make me more beautiful.
He took some moles off
dyed my hair and changed it.
Without cutting it there was something he did
to the inside of my mouth.

A JOURNEY

In this black and white
the light-shadow of Grayson Matthews,
the two sides of his nature
caught in a colorless photograph,

in which he holds two women
with beautiful bellies.
He is dressed and they are nude.
He is a photographer

and they are no one, anonymous
as beautiful stones. In the blurs
their eyes are gone but their hair
has turned to moonlit water.

Grayson is much taller and moves backwards
pulling them by the waists and shoulders.
His eyes are closed, and one hand
from one of them

closes his mouth, but he presses
his lips into her fingers and
sucks like someone whistling.
The women are violently off balance;
his pulling
is a sure photographer's pull.

Now they appear as a period piece.
Their heat is gone. They have the expressions
and the clothes of people in the 1960's.
Other photographers, more scientific

can move light meters across the image
to see if anything has changed the light,
if modern skies are darker. The women
struggle like blurred white birds

their legs and arms double exposed, kitty-cornered.
Their hunter, stealthy in his black sweater
moves one foot behind the heel of another
so as not to lose the force of his step.

GRAYSON'S PHOTOGRAPH

There is a boat out on the sea,
its image cast into a room.
Apricots as black as stones
and forks and medicine
just below it on a table
where it hangs flat as a blade of paper
the autumn light burning it.
The boat not moving.

Its pale gray rider still, and the water
turning to bear's breath and snow
as the apricots row with slight motion
and the forks click like insects.

The rower asks his imagination
and his mind opens like a black room
with medicines on the table
and old potatoes and lost salt.

Two shakers of lost salt from a neighbor's house
and curtains that draw in their stomachs.
There is no back to the room.
It is pale gray

and catches the light from the gray sea.
In that light you see a man
happy in his boat, drifting
out of the room

As the dead fruit dwindles to pits.

POWER

1. After Wayne and I
   walk Shadow through the Queen Anne's lace
   and it is stuck to every part of him
   like dry wedding veils
   we return to the housedust
   and fall into the bedroom
   two near drunk people;
   we separate into sleep.
   I dream of reincarnation in a perfect body
   blond as open vowels.
   I am much taller,
   a silver swimming pool, food and voices
   appear and like the excellent
   I taste people and let them go.
   Though I understand with my mind that they are people
   I have no human uses for them.
   Sex is a form of tennis, hot and jerky
   immediate like hot color.
   White costumes and motion fill my body.
   So this is the life of the privileged
   weird and plum-colored sleep
   no sensitivities, each moment blossoming.
   I peel off the tennis whites
   beside the pool, a new place in childhood,
   everything a noun, door, wall, sunshine, iris,
   others are bodies, only bodies, their motions, and forms
   exaggerated, and stylish.

2. After they had talked a while
   someone turned to the old Swedish woman and asked
   "Mother, at what age,
   does the man lose interest in sex?"
   and she answered them in Swedish, "Never,"
   softly, "never."
   By the white column of the house there is a mallow hybiscus
   not like the ordinary kind, much bigger,
   as if the hand of a Renaissance painter had extended it.

46

These beautiful days
and long language moving out of my body.
as the big girls move out of the house
and back into it,
maybe only to feed the animals.

I had a friend who was nervous
I want to tell you her name
though I shouldn't it was Evelyn North.
She could paint, anytime afterwards
anything she had seen.
But she also remembered
all her father's harsh words.
Goose-bodied, snow-faced
she had a kind of beauty, Dutch,
domestic, the beauty of longing.
Yet this embarrassed me
she used to get on the commute trains and just ride
saying those beautiful people were beautiful,
but they needed her to see them.

If there are gods they must want not
to be like us;
they know they are desired.
It is noiselessness
they want
that will not
let them sense us.

Honor Johnson was born in Alexandria, Louisiana. She earned her degrees at the University of Texas and the San Francisco Art Institute. In addition to being a writer, she is a painter and print maker. A first collection of poems *Herbal* was published last year by the Heyeck Press. She shared with Kathryn Terrill the 3rd Annual Anne Sexton Poetry Prize in 1979. She is married to Wayne Johnson. They live in Redwood City, California.